Two girls swirl their wide fiesta skirts in the exhaust of a rumbling bus. "Remember us? Remember us?" they shout to the poet who is crossing the street. "We were the best poets in the whole wide world! Did you keep our poems?"

SALTING
THE OCEAN

100 POEMS BY YOUNG POETS

SELECTED BY NAOMI SHIHAB NYE

PICTURES BY ASHLEY BRYAN

GREENWILLOW BOOKS
An Imprint of HarperCollinsPublishers

To the poets, the champions, with love,
& to my stunning editor, Virginia Duncan—N. S. N.

For Naomi's parents, dear friends
Miriam & Aziz Shihab—A.B.

The individual poets represented in this volume hold the copyrights to their poems.
Wherever possible, permission to reprint the poems has been obtained from the
individual poets, and the compiler and publisher gratefully acknowledge their
assistance. The scope of this volume made it occasionally difficult—despite sincere
and sustained effort—to locate poets and/or their executors. The compiler and
editor regret any omissions or errors and will make any necessary corrections in
subsequent printings.

The section titles in this book are memorable lines that have stayed with me over
the years. Grateful acknowledgment is given to the following young poets: Sam
Sanford for Section 1, Madelynn Mabry for Section 2, Eric Who-never-wrote-his-
last-name for Section 3, and Barbara Gonzales for Section 4.—N. S. N.

Tempera paints were used for the full-color art. The text type is Horley O.S.
Salting the Ocean : 100 Poems by Young Poets
Copyright © 2000 by Naomi Shihab Nye. Illustrations copyright © 2000
by Ashley Bryan. All rights reserved. No part of this book may be used or
reproduced in any manner whatsoever without written permission except in
the case of brief quotations embodied in critical articles and reviews.
Manufactured in China by South China Printing Company Ltd.
For information address HarperCollins Children's Books, a division of
HarperCollins Publishers, 1350 Avenue of the Americas, New York, NY 10019.
http://www.harperchildrens.com

Library of Congress Cataloging-in-Publication Data
Salting the ocean : 100 poems by young poets / poems selected by
Naomi Shihab Nye ; pictures by Ashley Bryan.
    p.   cm.
"Greenwillow Books."
ISBN 0-688-16193-6
[1. School verse, American.   2. Children's writings, American.   3. American
poetry—20th century.]   I. Nye, Naomi Shihab.   II. Bryan, Ashley, ill.
PS591.S3S19   2000   811'.540809282—dc21   99-30590   CIP
6 7 8 9 10   First Edition

A Note about the Poems

After her graduation from Trinity University in 1974, Naomi Shihab Nye began working as a writer-in-the-schools throughout the state of Texas via the Texas Commission on the Arts. She visited dozens of schools in small towns and cities to work with students and their writing. Later she worked extensively in Maine, Wyoming, and Oregon. Nye has also been a visiting writer at the University of California at Berkeley, the University of Hawaii at Manoa, the University of Texas at Austin and San Antonio, and the University of Alaska at Fairbanks. She continues to visit schools whenever possible and has led classroom poetry workshops in many of the fifty states. The poems in this book were selected from the vast heaps that she has saved from her classes over the past twenty-five years and represent students in grades 1–12.

CONTENTS

AN INTRODUCTION IN 3 PARTS

like a dance, like a sandwich . . .

What does a word want?
My words want to talk to me.
Words empty me out at night.
    —*Hannah Elizabeth Carter*

To Anyone, and to a Couple in Nova Scotia

Twenty-two years old, fresh out of college and touring Canada on my own, I dialed hotel phone numbers from a telephone booth in Halifax, Nova Scotia. Chilly rain poured down outside. Where would I sleep that night? The youth hostel was full. Every hotel, full. En route to the Canadian National Railroad station and a train that would take me over to Quebec the next day, I felt stranded. No one could have imagined it would be so hard to find a place to stay.

I felt tremulous about the future in general. That following autumn when I returned to Texas, I would begin working as a "writer-in-the-schools." What did a writer-in-the-schools do? Help students write. Try to inspire and encourage them. It sounded so—elemental, so grassroots, so—terrifying.

Although I had loved poetry since the age of six, had published poems since the age of seven, and had been working at a summer institute for teenage writers for four years, I had never taken a single education class, and had managed to whiz through my interview with the Texas Commission on the Arts for the mysterious position sans vita, references, or a single page of poetry. Was I dreaming? Was I doomed?

A man knocked on the door of the phone booth. "Are you okay? You've been in there—a really long time."

I cracked the door, shivering. "I'm sorry. Umm—every hotel in town is full. Do you happen to know any little place I might stay for just one night?"

The man motioned to a woman walking toward him. She carried a grocery bag under a wide umbrella. "Come with us," he said. "This is my wife, we live right down the street. You can sleep on our couch."

It was 1974. I followed them. Drinking a cup of hot tea in their cozy living room, he said, "So what do you do?" When I said, "I'll be working with writing and kids . . ." he handed me a copy of *Wishes, Lies and Dreams* by Kenneth Koch, who'd been doing similar work with kids in New York City. The paperback had just come out. "Take it," the man said. "It looks great. Read it on the train. Good luck!"

I started reading that night, by the light of an old-fashioned lamp, and felt a warmth and belief rise up inside that have abided for decades, one century easing miraculously into another, poetry more necessary than ever as a fire to light our tongues. I did not get that couple's address and could never thank them in writing till now. The book *was* great. It heartened me immeasurably in those early working days. I read it again and again and still have my tattered copy along with whole shelves of books now available on the subject. After conducting thousands of classes in inner-city schools and far-flung rural locations, I could—as most of us could, who have discovered this work—still do another one tomorrow.

To Teachers, Librarians, Parents, and Other Friends
Who May Pick Up This Book

In the midst of public jabber, high-velocity advertising, and shameless television, where is one true word? Where are three? Who will pause long enough to describe something truly, and clearly? Where is the burn of speech, the sweet rub of language, the spark that links us?

Poetry, poetry! Rearranging right at the heart level, where standardized tests often don't go. I think our frenzied days are hungry for the kind of quietude poetry offers. It doesn't take long to weave it into our lives.

Recently I led a discussion about poetry for a "Parents' Night" at our son's school. One mother stared at me with encouraging interest. At the end of the session, after everyone had warmed up and written and shared their work and laughed, she raised her hand. "You came to my school when I was in high school, and we did just what we did tonight—heard poems, talked, wrote our own, read them out loud—and after you left, we kids missed that experience terribly. We realized we had never had a chance really to *listen* to one another before those poetry sessions, and now they were over. We'd been going to school for so long! Why didn't we get to hear one another's real voices and thoughts more often?"

Saying this years later, she burst into tears.

It was a perfect cap for our evening.

"How should we use poetry?" people sometimes ask me. Read it! Share it with one another! Find poems that make you resonate. Different poems will do this for every person. We "use poetry" to restore us to feeling, revitalize our own speech, awaken empathy.

There are many things we may come to know about poetry, but some of the initial essences stay the same; it's a portable, intimate genre, pocket-sized, which should make it quickly inviting in a classroom setting. A poem's size grants us time to read and reread. A poem wants to be read aloud, as our poet laureate Robert Pinsky has reminded us with his "Favorite Poems" project. Use a poem at the beginning or end of a class. Put a poem on the board and don't even discuss it—let it permeate the atmosphere on its own.

Poems sometimes invite a spectrum of interpretations that help extend us as readers, thinkers, and speakers. We may like a poem without understanding everything about it. People have spent way too much time trying to "explain" poetry when it has always been the most intuitive, suggestive genre. Do we explain music every time we listen to it? Mystery remains part of many poems, as well it should, since it remains part of our lives no matter who or where we are.

There may be nothing more "basic" in education than gaining a sense of one's own voice. By acknowledging and shaping shared experience, we grow bigger. Poems help us see the world around us as rich material. And nothing is better than reading the work of our peers, as well as the work of older poets, to get us going in our particular terrain. A poem we love makes us want to write our own—hand to hand, map to map, contagious, delicious voices spinning us forward inside our cluttered, clattering lives.

I vote with Paul Slattery of San Antonio who wrote:

> "What goes through your head
>   when you stare at a blank space?
>   Nothing to write about, you may say.
>   Nothing to write for.
>   If you think, you can write.
>   If you live, you can write.
>   If you think nothing, write nothing.
>   If you do live, then spell with your heart."

To the Poets

Thank you. Thank you for not being too shy to say things. Thank you for experimenting. One of the first discoveries I made about writing a poem was that I felt strangely satisfied after doing it, as if my brain had gathered its loose, raggedy threads, woven them together, and calmed down. Having done something with what I had seen and heard, now I could move on to think about other things. Sometimes writing a poem even helped me see what I was thinking about, or helped me pay better attention to details. Writing a poem was not separate from living, it was more like *Living Twice*. If someone else read my words and understood them, or felt closer to their own thoughts in some way, that was an extra gift.

Basically, here's my advice: *take time*.

In your life, you may always feel as if you don't have enough time. Adults are specialists at feeling that. Strangely, writing seems to give us a deeper sense of our own time and *time* in general.

What do we need? A quiet minute, a pencil, a page. Notebooks are good for keeping pages together. Please be kind to yourself when you write. Don't expect you will love everything that comes out—let *many* things come out, and know that now and then you will like a line or a phrase enough to let it carry you away. Don't be stingy! Don't write just a few lines and think that's all you have to say. But a few lines are better than none. It's better to write a little bit every day than wait for a perfect empty day to come along, because it won't. Start where you are. A few lines before bedtime, at least. Or a few lines right after you wake up or after school.

Be patient and generous as often as you can. Get in the habit of welcoming your own words, however slowly or quickly they come to you. If you feel you don't have any "ideas" (sometimes the worst thing you can do as a writer is wait for a "great idea" to come along) then write down some questions you carry. Some bits and pieces. Some "wisps," as my favorite poet, William Stafford, used to say. "Hints."

My friend Ralph Fletcher has said there may be many things that are "too big" to write about in their entirety, but there is nothing too small. If you start with something small, it may carry you toward something wider.

You are making a map of the days you live.

No one can predict what will happen when you start paying attention to and enjoying your own words on the page. But I can promise you one thing: whatever you do in your life, whatever path you follow, if you are a person who feels comfortable writing your own words down, you will have an easier, better time of everything.

Language will befriend you in more ways than you can guess. Even little things like writing a thank-you note will feel easier when writing becomes a relaxed habit. And you will always have someone to talk to—yourself, on a page. If you have to give a speech or compose a memo, you'll know how to do it. Your powers of remembering and noticing will be exercised and honored again and again.

I wish you well and thank you for your wonderful voices.

Naomi Shihab Nye
San Antonio, Texas, 2000

"My Shadow Is an Ant's Night"

THE SELF AND THE INNER WORLD

thirty-two poems

Cabbage

Cabbage is like a
folded-up flower all
tight and closed
up from the world
or like an artichoke.
Why are you
closed up
from the world,
why?
You tell me that
everyone is closed up
from the world?
No, that's not true.
Here. Let me help you
open your leaves,
oh leafy one.

 John Mullins

3

The words just jumped
into the quiet.

The words blasted
into the dark.

 Seth Hansford

I like to:

collect rocks on Venus
dance on Mars
eat on Pluto
buy rings on Saturn
ride a bike to Mercury
swim in the desert
write in fire

Jeffrey Trevino

When I Was Born

When I was born,
it was like a big ocean
with one fish.

Then it was like
I was not the only one
in the ocean.

And when I was bigger,
it was like an elephant
in a jar.

Homer Soto

Song of My Foot

I sing about my right foot.
I sing about it because
my favorite shoe goes on that foot.
I sing about my right shoe because
it is old and the shoelace is torn.
I sing about my shoelace because
it is stained with dirt and mud.
I sing about dirt and mud because
it is part of this world.

 Marci Carlson

About My Body

My eyes are like marbles rolling
around inside my head.
The water inside me is like a
deep, deep ocean with sharks, fish
jumping up and down.
The water might be cold to them,
but it's not to me.
And I think there's a whale inside me
now.
When I think of them, I
always want to take
their pictures.
So I will just call to them.
Say cheese, then snap.
I got the picture of a giant whale.

 Hays Butler

I saw happiness on my front doorstep.
I heard sadness in my backyard.
I met scaredness in the park.
I found madness way high in a tree.
And all my life they've followed me.

Margo Bierwirth

How to Grow Up

1. Take yourself and go to sleep like
   Sleeping Beauty.

2. Sleep for 3 to 6 years.

3. When you wake up check your age.
   If it isn't right go to sleep again.
   If you can't go to sleep try this.

1. Take a growing pill made of sassafras
        and bullwinkle mixed together with beetle juice.

2.   Buy the pill at the Children's Dream Shop.
        It costs $15 for one pill.

3. After taking the pill sit in a very large chair
        with the age you want to be painted on,
            put your pinkies in your eyes
                and count to 1,000 by halves.
        Wait an hour and I think
            you'll be the age
                you want
                    to be.

If not nothing will help.

Alison Sagebiel

When I'm at Home on Sunday Alone

I feel like a lonesome house
that no one wants to live in
or like a skunk that no one
wants to play with
and I hear funny noises
like voices of uncles that died
and when my friends come
I don't feel lonesome anymore
but when they leave
I feel like a tree that died.

Freddy Galvan

It's Inside of Me!

The movement of
rivers is in me.
In my blood.
The smartness of Einstein
is in me.
In my head.
The stillness of rocks
is in me.
In my body.
The color of trees
is in me.
In my skin.
The looseness of dirt
is in me.
In my bones.
The fastness of rabbits
is in me.
In my legs.
The seeing of eagles
is in me.
In my eyes.

The neatness of cats
is in me.
In my hands.
That is me.

Adam Delavan

Remember

I remember when I was little,
my father said,
"Are you sure this is our baby?
This looks like a Spanish baby."

I remember when I was in first grade,
everyone was on page 189
and I was on
page 1.

 Gloria Rabel

I feel like a puppy that
can't catch up to his mother.
Like a creek that runs fast
but can't reach the ocean.
Like a runner who stays all day
in the starting line.
My mind is like an empty box.

Time like a racing car
running at the speed of light.

 Alberto Santillana

I am a girl.
I am a sweet girl.
I am a helpful girl.
I am a shy little girl.
I feel like a chained-up little elephant
in a zoo.

 Bonnie Gutierrez

Ode to My Size

I sing to the size I am,
small and a black-haired person.
There are two boys and two girls
that are taller than me.
And when they pass by me I wish,
I wish I was tall myself.
I sing the size of me and my
companion that sits beside me. We
are both small but he is a little bigger
than me but I don't care about that.
I am just glad that I am a person.

Peter Acosta

Monday Mornings

On Monday mornings I feel like
a miserable mouse, more miserable
than a monkey on Monday mornings.

On Monday mornings I feel like
a miserable midget, more miserable
than a glass of milk or a mommy.

On Monday mornings I feel like
a miserable millionaire, more miserable
than money, more miserable than
midnight.

 Pauline Alva

Letter to Myself

My hair always stands up like a witch.
My hair stinks like a mop in dirty water.
I feel like a rabbit is taking a bath
in my stomach.
My bones feel so hot and so cold.
I want to tell my arms
to run away and go to heaven.

Christine Ramirez

I am . . .

an unpredictable topsy-turvy jester for a king who can't laugh.
an eleven-year-old that makes up in intelligence what
he lacks in wisdom.
dust in the vacuum cleaner.
a ball rolling inside of a hollow doughnut.
an armless Mickey Mouse watch.
a flag without a country.
the cellar of an underground house.
a balloon that is continually being deflated and blown-up
again by a porcupine.
things that I will never be able to know or even guess.

 Jason Witherspoon

I had a yellow daffodil.
I put it in a vase of fresh water.
The vase broke and water spilled everywhere.
My flower fell, I put it in a pot in my window.
It wilted.

I had a beautiful bird.
I put it in a cage of gold.
It didn't sing.
I put it in a birdhouse.
It flew away over the waters.

I had a painted picture of a lady.
She was dressed in silk.
The picture tore, it was burned.

I dream about them, my treasures.

Nicole Batey

My Mind Is an Empty Jug

I wonder where it went.

In the morning I felt like
an empty jug so I felt
my pillow it was not wet
but my mind was empty

I wonder where it went.

Alex Lagunas

One

We had a
"Most commonly misspelled word"
Spelling test
Yesterday in English,
Fourth Period.
I commonly misspelled them all.
Except one.
Loneliness
was the only one I got right.

Butch McElroy

I sing deep songs.
I fly like a river on the wind.
I dance like dreamer corner.
I remember the star like loose white jagged bones.
I open darkness like snow on a chicken.
I shout like an empty sail in the air.
I bounce like a broken ribbon on a window chime.
I sparkle like the golden road.

Dillard Yates

Help. Or, You Are Your Own Oasis.

The bones hang limp and you rearrange them.
You knit the ends of the fingers closed.
You breathe and pray the breath stays tight in the body.
That is about all you can do—one final step:
you re-light the candle behind the eyes—it sucks
at the wax like a new baby at its mother.
You cannot do more. You hope he knows
that each person sustains himself every day,
like making the bed, tucking the sheets extra tight;
that each person has his own rhythms caught in his body,
from these he learns to dance—from nothing else,
    from nothing more—
that each person has his own life, when you cup
your hands together and blow into them,
the echoes will tell journeys and episodes from this life.
Each one moving with a scaly covering,
each fish moving toward others separated by the water
    in between,
the air breathed in must go out,
each alone in the desert of his body,
each one singing, guitar dug low into his belly.

Christy Walker

Our Spirits

The river sizzles down
like the color of a dissolved stoplight.
Our memory ripples away from us
like a stretched shadow.
Spirits, voices inside ourselves,
dissolve into puddles of open roses.
We try to grasp the world inside ourselves
but it slips away like a spoon in fog.

Tanya Naumer

I looked into a drop
of water. I saw nothing.
But I also saw everything.
I couldn't make out quite
everything or nothing
but I knew that it was
something.

I looked into a cool
shallow pond. But
this time I could
see everything and
I could see nothing.

Nothing was a cold
and damp space that
was deep at the bottom
of the pond. Everything skimmed
across the top of the water
full of joy and bright colors.

Then everything and
nothing came together
and I saw my reflection.

 Luke Bennett

On Friday, my face, a new-bloomed
flower, my teeth, big bright stars,
my heart, a budding red rose,
my future, an unpredictable rabbit,
my blood, a flowing red river,
when home, my happiness,
an everlasting sky.

Arthur Lee Childress

Sandra is like
a flower.
No one knows she
dances with the wind and
remembers
about when she was just coming out
of the ground.

Sandra Perez

Anonymous

I am anonymous.
I am only known to a
small group.
The world doesn't know
    ME.
My future doesn't know
    ME.
Sometimes I am not known to my
    PARENTS.
My insides don't know my outsides.
I am only known to some things but not many.
I AM ANONYMOUS.

 Christopher D. Viner

We all float in and out.
I floated into Humanities
and I will probably float to my break
and I will probably float out.
I don't know why I float.
I don't care,
I like floating.
If the world's population floated,
life would be more hopeful.
But I don't like to be lonely.
I bet everybody in here is lonely for something.
Me, I'm lonely for comfort.
She's probably lonely for her cat,
he for his basketball court.
Colors are nice.
I'm glad the world is in color.
I wish one color didn't exist though.
Institution green,
Any green but that.

Kathryn Cuma

The Storm in Me

I have a storm in me
and a muddy heart and
a broken bone I have a raining brain and a
turned over car I wish I didn't have a storm in me

      Sadness in my body

I have a sadness in me
and a sad stomach and
a broken brain I have lonely teeth I wish there
wasn't sadness in my life ever again

Theresa Ann Garcia

Patterns

Wherever I stand, I hear the trees petition.
—William Stafford

I think of how the rain
is washing life away.

How do I know what life
has in store for me?

It is strange that I cannot
figure out the pattern.

The trees are so perfect,
they know how to grow.

Leticia Gray

When I was born
I was a Ugly red
head baby boy.
The world was
big but I only
mattered. My brother
was the giant and
I was the midget.
I got bigger and
bigger and the
world seemed
to get smaller
and smaller.
Maybe someday
it will be the
size of a penny
and I could put it
in my pocket
and walk to the sunset.

Rusty Nye

I have a rock in me
that flows over storms and rain
when earthquakes come
it sometimes wants to crack
but the ocean givin' it the courage
to go on, on and on forever . . .

I have a heart key in me
that loves like mother
that cries like baby
that sings like a patriot
that's cracky like a rocking chair . . .

I have an owl in me
that loves when darkness comes
that can turn its head any way it please
that watch, when no one is there
that love to see the beautiful
    moonshine in darkness . . .

I have an old chair in me
that no one wants to sit in
that keeps dust on it
that gets thrown around . . .
but the chair is *worthy* . . .

I have an empty box in me
that wants to be filled with lots of loving dolls
that needs a music box in it
that has a moonlight corner
that has a little pick of sunlight in it . . .

I have a dark barn in me that is filled with talent
that is bubbling over with hay but no one has room for it
that has bumping and green trees and mountains
and beautiful blue sky all around . . .

I have a secret closet in me that is wide open
        and no one can see . . .
that has a secret lovebird who doesn't know when
        to sing the song . . .
sometimes be lucky to see a little moonlight
and a happy baby together with its toys . . .

I have a superstar in me . . .
It may not shine when I want it to
it may not go down when I want it to
but a lonely lovable superstar
is what it takes to get along
this dangerous night.

Rachel Moore (excerpted from a longer poem)

"Think How Many Stories Are in Your Shirt"

WHERE WE LIVE

~ *twenty poems*

My Street

bright and shiny   straight and crooked
and clean sidewalks and
designs of animals and people
trees beside the sidewalk
hills and mountains
and the most important
is myself
great things around the street
street that leads to the city
stores and buildings
nice kittens around
the street
and houses and dogs
and barkingful wonder
buildings
and houses
roosters around my house and other houses
who
do you think
I
am am am
?

Jesus Alarcon, Jr.

Inside Out

My brother's socks
    Inside out
My brain
    Inside out
The world
    Inside out
My jacket
    Inside out
The sky
    Inside out
Darkness
    Inside out

Wayne Anderson

On Leal Street

A man passes at ten p.m.
He is very tall like a tree
He has a voice like talking
    in a cave
And when the man passes
the trees close in like
    rainbows

Joann Caballero

Gliding

Sometimes I am a dog blooming in the sky
and sometimes I am the wind going across the world
but most of all I am a boy who runs
and in my house I am just a boy sleeping
or lying across my bed.

*

gliding
gliding
when I glide I feel
like a bird
blooming
across the sky
like an eagle catching fish
I glide
by my house
singing
hearing the ocean
whhh   whhh

Noel Guzman

For My First-Grade Teacher

I remember the time you told me
to zip my lip
I remember the time you made
popcorn for the
whole class
I remember the time when you made
me and some
other kids
stand in
front
of the
class
But now it doesn't matter at all
because
I
don't see
you
anymore

Rachel Obregon

Where We Live

My mom is asking for garlic from our neighbor.
She gives it to her.
My mom puts the garlic in the rice.
My dad comes home. He is very hungry.
We all run up to greet him.
We sit to have supper.
My brother says grace.
We watch TV after supper.
9:00 p.m. we go to bed.
6:00 a.m. get ready for school.
7:00 a.m. David takes his medicine.
7:05 a.m. leave for school.
3:00 p.m. come home from school.
My mom asks me to pay the neighbor back her garlic.

Amy Gonzales

The Olehehe

I think of mountains. Some
mountains have snow but this one
doesn't. I go on top of the mountain and yell
Olehehe. I like when the mountain
echoes me

    Olehehe
    Olehehe
    Olehehe

It is really rocky and when you
yell, watch out the rocks will start falling.
Echo me, mountain

    Olehehe
    Olehehe
    Olehehe

Come on, mountains, echo me.
Echo me, you can do better
than that, echo me

Olehehe
Olehehe
Olehehe

Linda White

Silver moon shooting bullets at you from the sky
landing right in your pocket very gently.

Raymond Lopez

The World

The trees are like the hair of the world.
The city is like the heart of the world.
The wind is a flute player
playing in the night.
The cars beeping horns are like buttons
beeping inside the earth.
Each bird is like a single piccolo
singing away
and the grass, just like me,
being buried under the snow.

Noel Berry

Winter

In winter the city snow turns golden.
In·winter the coolness crackles
and burns in the fireplace.
The moon looks like steel in the sun.
The air is cold outside.
Children dream of snow bullets.
They see a wizard in the mirror.
The snow bullets form a wave.
The river freezes.
The star smiles.

 Sean Cassidy

Loneliness

A man is swimming down
   below.
He looks like a swell fellow,
   a man
reading on the catwalk
   and a maid
mopping up a spilled mess.
   A woman
entering her apartment after
a hard day's work. While a man
& woman look at a map about
to go to the Nile. Busy cars
      moving
by. A man almost stepped in some
      tar.
It's so quiet and peaceful. Just
      think
right this second a war's going
      on.

A TV ad said It's a
   shame to waste a brain.
      Everything's
going on at once. As the months
go flying by.

 Richard Wolf

Friend Sounds

ext door my friend sister be crying.
She cries like this   wa wa.
When her father comes in her big sister
get in trouble. She cries like this   hm hm.
Her brother cries like this   Moo Moo.
Her mother screams and her father
yells.

 Laurice Roy

Rules for Trees

1. No holding branches.
2. No touching roots.
3. No losing your leaves.
4. Keep your tree straight.

Dana Scharein Dague

What happened to my cat?
His glittery eyes
no longer look upon me
while I slumber or toil over my human problems.

I miss his sweet face
tinged with light brown
and a snowy sugary white
that always seemed to be smiling to fill me with love.

I miss stroking his soft fur
while he listlessly sunned
every day on the windowsill
even when it rained and we covered him to keep him warm.

His eyes were a mixture
of topaz, water, and the sky
and when he looked at you,
you couldn't help but wonder what he was thinking.

He was a cat,
he was love,
he was like a cloud in the sky,
and like a cloud in the sky
he has floated away.

Jennifer D. Caraway

The Jungle

Birds are gathering together
for the last time to eat
dinner near my window.
They sit around and pass bird seeds
to each other for another something to receive.

During the winter the grass sounds
like bacon frying with a pot of grease.

In the fall the leaves drop
like dry snowflakes in the summer.

Branches swing from side to side
like your mother is chasing you
with a switch for not doing the dishes.

Trees sound like
running water
year after year.

Portia Gentry Carrington

As I walk in the moonlight
I sing of darkness,
I sing of clouds,
of big black clouds,
how they change like people,
they meet and they flee.

I sing of people, rainbow's light,
of empty roads and wooded nights.
My voice is deep.
It sparkles to your ears
and swirls dust away.
My voice flaps and moves
like a river.
It whispers to the world,
sometimes it shouts,
but yet it has a heart.
My voice can be a swan
and speak with its wings,
but behind it is a shadow
that looks like the world.

Vangie Castillo

Incantation for the Loved One

I will be walking through the dirt streets.
I will notice every detail of the roads
and will pick a flower from the pond.
I will bury the flower in the sand.

Two days later I will come
and if the flower has not dried yet,
I will say to the sea,
"May the love that you once felt for me
never die like this flower.
May you always feel the same way toward me,"
and after I say that, I will again walk home.

 Elsa Perales

On My Roof

Looking at
Stars on the roof,
Wondering if we are the
Only beings with superior
Intelligence in this vast emptiness.
Each star is like our sun,
With some bigger,
Some smaller.
Some already dead and gone.
Like I will be
Someday.

Except it won't take hundreds
Of years for my
Image to
Disappear.

Raúl Alfonso Cadena

Monday Night at Kwik-Wash

Lady with broad back, glasses, and
Pepto-pink polish
Glistening on her nails.
Looks bored.
What's she thinking?
I wonder.
Mr. Clock swinging his arms swiftly.
Mrs. Dryer warm and soothing,
Hugging and kissing my clothes.
Palm under my chin,
Fingers galloping steadily
On my cheek.
I watch the fuzzy lights
Bounce off the glass
Painted by anxious drivers.
Colors whirl
Thoughts swirl
When will my freedom come?

 Rebecca Martinez

Mart dreams that
America is as beautiful as a
    newly washed
Rabbit with his hair
    glistening in
The moon's light.
In the dream everything
    is old-fashioned.
      There are no robbers or
      terrorists.
Newly fallen snow shines
    in the light. Then I
    wake up, it was the
    middle of the night.
    I still love America.

Mart Thaggard

"My Grandma Squashes Roaches with Her Hand"

ANYBODY'S FAMILY

❧ *twenty-three poems*

My name came from my great-great-great-grandfather.
He was an Indian from the Choctaw tribe.
His name was Dark Ant.
When he went to get a job out in a city
he changed it to Emmett.
And his whole name was Emmett Perez Tenorio.
And my name means: Ant; Strong; Carry twice
its size.

Emmett Tenorio Meléndez

My Grandma's Tree

My grandma has a tree that cries
like a lovely moon hearing the sunshine.
My grandma's tree has a smell like a rose.
The roses that my grandma sees make
her tree turn into lightning   just like
Dr. Frankenstein's machine.
My grandma has a tree that cries
like a man having his honeymoon
          with his wife,
or like a lady that goes outside
and looks at the sea   when she has
        her first romance.

Sylvia Gomez

Alone with my mirror,
Dreaming of love,
Wishing for love,
Thinking of my dear old grandmother.
My eyes represent my grandmother.
My nose represents my grandmother.
Suddenly my face turns into my
Dear old grandmother.
I start to speak.
I hear my voice
I hear my grandmother's voice
I say to myself, "That can't
be my grandmother, she is dead."
She says to me, "It *is* your grandmother."
I had trust in my grandmother so
I believe my grandmother lives
beyond death, in my mirror.

 Brenda L. Burmeister

My father
a volcano
ready to explode
My mother
a roaring lion
My sister
King Kong destroying
buildings
A little girl but with a
big fist
And I
an ant stuck in a
coffin

Ernest Beache

For My Grandmother

She was massive in her old furs
and coffee-stained smiles,
and her words were stone,
but she liked parades
and she bit into them like
inevitable fruits.

John Phillip Santos

My Grandfather

My grandfather tells me things
I never heard.
When he is sick, I hear him cry.
I try to help him, but when I get there,
he turns well.

My grandfather walks alone.

And when he comes back, he tells me a story
which gets into my heart and stays there
like a diamond in a ring.

That's my grandfather, a faithful man.

 Alfonso Vargas

Pictures

There are three windows in my room.
Nobody understands
my windows unless they
see them.

One holds
the entire upper floor
of my mother's
scarlet Japanese maple
tree.
And some of the backyard
and the snow-white
garden gate
wedged between the overly
abundant green hedge.

Another window frames
the tightrope
where my bushy-tailed
acrobat friends
scurry along,
giving no thought to the fact

that down below awaits
not a circus net,
but a sidewalk.

My third window
can be my favorite
when I look down to see
my father
and mother
in the early morning sun
sitting on the patio
with their cups
of coffee.

Lori Herrell

In the Morning

i wake up
5:30 am

before my mother
before my brothers
before my sisters

i wake up
5:30 am

to a silent house
in a silent room
to a silent morning

—wake up
5:30 am

leave the house
6:20 am

before the yelling
before the screaming
before the pain

i wake up
5:30 am

to a silent house
in a silent room
to a silent morning.

Mary Gutierrez

My Dad

My father sails he sails
in his sleep he sails when he's awake
I think he falls asleep by listening
to the waves hit the hull of his imaginary boat
and the sail clanging against the mast
I love my father I know he will
fall asleep and never awake
but I will be happy because he
will still be sailing in his lake

William V. Lange

When I used to go to the beach
my mother would take a saltshaker
and make the water salty

With great expertise
she would taste, salt, taste
and salt again
five minutes or so
until she decided it was right

Then I would go swimming
thinking my mother
salted the whole ocean
however large it was

I now know
my mother isn't responsible
for the salty ocean

It takes some of the fun
out of going to the beach

 Bill Collins

The mean is on me.
The family is on me.
The eyes of a dragon are on me.
The scream of my brother is on me.
The smoke of the chimney is on me.
The school is on me.
The wall is on me.
Well everything is on me, I don't know
why. Anyway I'm gonna get
on them too, like they got on me.

I'm gonna scream on them.
I'm gonna be mean on them.
Well I'm gonna do everything
they did to me.

 Veronica Samaniego

A Charm to Get My Dad to Come Back

Whenever I want my dad
to come back all I say is
  come-a
  come-a
  come-a
and then I see him
with my mother and then I
play catch with him and when
it's time to bring him back
all I say is
  come-a
  come-a
  come-a and then
he's here and I wish I had
a charm to make him stay
forever.

Richard Delacruz

I remember me
   as a ladybug.
Now my parents have caught me.
I have Sisters and Brothers.
Now
   they are ladybugs.
We are flying
   together.
We are all caught by
   people.

Amy Briggs

My mother is a shell
and you can always hear
the ocean.

Brenda Garcia

First Love

Her hands are road maps to get to another world
Her hair is the weeds in a garden
Her hair is a bird's nest all alone as dark as
a winter night sky as light as a white cloud
drifting in the sky waiting for someone else
Her heart a key to the door that comes next
and the one after that and the one after that
and the next one also
Her hands will guide you to the doors
Her heart will get you through them
Her hair will give you space to live once you get there
but you have to be careful one wrong turn
and she will disappear and you must start over again
you must remember you must be wise
for things do not come back
It is important to know what happened
for she will disappear anyway
so let her hands guide you
let her heart get you through the door
and let her hair give you space
and use it well for there is not much time
she will disappear soon and help others also

Joanna Lang Winslade

Rounding Up the Stars

I would put them
in a jar
and make a light
out of it
and I would go get it
right now if you'd
let me
and I would
give it to my mom
for a Christmas present
and she would
let me use it too
and together
we would
read with it.

 Jerry L. Middlebrook

Mimi

My Mimi never got mad.
She would welcome you
happily.
She was good at many things
but mostly
being nice.
A manger scene
by her big brick fireplace,
and a colorful parrot magnet . . .
she walked about
like she was confused.
She was sweet singing
and old carpet.
She smelled of
perfume.
I was cleansed water
from a rocky stream.
My Mimi never got mad.
She is happy above
watching everyone.
I was afraid to give her
the picture I colored for her birthday

in fear she knew
I thought she would die in four days.
But she knew.
She has now spread throughout my mind
so she pops up in every thought.
But now
I can't tell her
everything
anymore.

 Rachel Dealy

Horizons
have torn
years
and people.

 Michelle Heintz

Nana

Nana,

who dreams of her new house,

who sleeps in a nightcap made of
silk,

who worries about herself,

who is lonely. And talks to
the moon. Lonely Grandma
move to the city. Be happy
with people. Be able to walk
long ways with a new friend.

Who is lonely and seems
like she says 50 words
a minute.

Who is scared and alone all
day till 6:00 when Daddy
Lynn gets home. Be neat,
sort through, and you'll be
new. I love you, too.

 Rosalynn Dugger

Grandmother

How old were you before you
were old enough to go out on your own?

My granddaughter,
I was never ready to go out
in the world all alone.

 Sandra Scherbenske

Marbles

My mother has this amazing talent;
she launches her fears to scatter in my room.
She projects them with the tip of her nose
her voice on the telephone
and the soft muscles of her mouth.

Little spies; they warn me of nightmare deadlines
application-essay grammar traps
and the tricks of entrance examinations.

They have gotten in.
I feel them rolling around in my head like marbles.
They speak with insistent voices, like zippers and
foghorns.

"Next year," they say, "away from here."
"Be good, be smart. Wear a hat in the sun.
Use a thesaurus. Make sure to blacken in
all those little boxes
with your #2 pencil."

    Am I growing up?
I begin to promise rather than ignore—
I address these marbles, one by one.
They don't rattle so much anymore.

And once yesterday I looked up
to see my mother smiling.

Sarah Lucille Fisch

My mother had a pet bird.
The name of the bird was Martin.
When a month had passed, my mother's bird had gone away.
My mother told my father to go after her bird.
My father was looking for the bird for a year.
My father said, "I will get old before my time."
And then when my mother had a baby, they went to the church to baptize the baby. And when the priest said,
"What are you going to name him?" my father said,
"MARTIN LEWIS SALAZAR period so I don't have to go look for the silly bird."

Martin Salazar

The Old Black Truck

I often think about the old black truck
The one that sat alone on my Grandpa's farm
The one my mom nearly died in—
The one my sister had a wreck in—
I kinda took a liking to that old truck
I was gonna fix it up a bit
It just needed a few minor changes
It supplied a home for little rabbits
Yes sir I was gonna fix that truck up
It would be jet black with a roll bar in back
It would have big slick tires just waiting to be set free
Then the news hit me
It was sold for a hundred dollars
I never felt sicker than the day they told me
Yes sir, that truck would have been the best around
But now it's gone for me and someone else
Had a dream come true.

Gary Ullmann

"SILENCE
IS LIKE A TRACTOR
MOVING
THE WHOLE WORLD"

THE WIDE IMAGINATION

twenty-five poems

Clock

Clock, who has looked at you
and seen the time?
Who has looked at you
and said they were late?
Clock, you must be tired,
after all, you stay up all night.
Clock, who has looked at you
and said they only had five minutes?
Clock, how many times
have you been wound?
Clock, you have all the time
in the world locked up inside.

Robert Kimmel

When I smile, my hair begins to chime
in the darkness.
When I faint, my arms turn black and blue
in the sunlight.
When I give birth to an idea, my stomach
starts to tingle in the clouds.
When I'm walking through the forest at night,
I hear the trees sing and the beaver run.

Peter Ramzy

I touched
the roughness
of my wrinkled paper
as I rumpled it
in my hands.

And remembered
as I rubbed the edges—
how life expands.

Cyndea L. Peacock

Mixed-Up Spring

The stone chases golden sunlight.
I chase the stone.
Sunlight crackles
and pebbles shine.

The trees gleam
and grass whistles.
Leaves bud
and flowers flow.
Bees burn
and metal stings.

Jessica Caitlin Zachary

Harvest your dreams.
Darkness is coming on
and the silence is almost deafening
in the stormy night.

Tammy Wiloth Brown

The Friday-Saturday Weekend

On free Friday I feel from
another free planet.
I feel like a four-faced monster
and five-fingered leopard.
Friday is a fine Friday
    four, five, fifteen-headed monster.
Friday is the fifth day of the week.

Friday is a special day.
The Saturday is special space.
Day   space   Saturday is a
special day because you go to the
store, soft pillow,
soft bed, everything is soft
in space   Saturday   space
Saturday sounds special   very special
sounds   space   sounds

Augustin Moreno

I hear a perfect sound about a bluejay.
I love morning sunrise going over the crisp cool sky.
I taste chocolate pie and double thick frosting.
I feel a soft warm mother beside me.
I touch a new bloomed rose.
I wish to have a thousand friends made up of bread and honey.
I think of a newborn baby belonging to my mother.
I hear my mother's call for miles away.
I love my aunts of the universe.
I believe in my mother's birth.

 Suchil Guerra

Charm to Bring Back the Past

I will risk my life to bring back the Past.
I will order it at a restaurant.
It will cost but it's worth it.
I will invite it to my house and treat it
as if it were my relative.
If the Past feels bad, I feel bad.
If the Past feels good, I feel good.
Sometimes I feel further back in the Past
than the Past itself.
I wish the Past would come back
so my older relatives would have those good times
they told me they had.
Please come back Past please come back.

 Martin Laureles

Pool of Mirrors

I saw a pool of mirrors

it looks in and back
from time to end

then it looks upon you
wondering what you are wondering
wondering what you are thinking
and feeling

you go over to it
and feel the pool
and it feels of crystal cold glass
and tastes of perfect honor
and perfect magic

the pool of mirrors
looks upon you

it glistens on the yesterdays

gleam of the honey sun

   Larry B. Springer, Jr.

Words,
jumbled
in my mind.
Traffic jams
of sentences,
swirling,
and bubbling,
in the cauldron of my mind.
All I can do
is think
and write.
Breathe deeply,
and let your feelings flow
onto the page.
Let your mind fill
with ideas.

Let them bolt
through your pencil,
crashing
with enormous
energy
onto your paper.
Poetry
has her own way of living.
Let her live
in peace.

Rachel M. Reynolds

The sky looks like the ocean.
The
flowers smell like perfume.
But
nobody's happy.

 Amy S. Arnold

Questions are boxes wrapped in paper.
When you remove the bright ones from the pile
you can see the simpler ones . . . the ones holding the
decorative ones up. When you open
the simplest boxes, you get the
best gifts.

Valerie Marie Vick

Spring feels like another three thorny months
full of moaning and groaning,
getting going, ready for subtle, sweat-smelling
Summer.
Spring moves along as if not caring how,
slipping, sliding. Summer rolls in.
Swimming in spring? What an unthinkable thing!
I couldn't show my face in the slimy
    swallowing present-tense
        of Spring.

Spring Odiorne

I Love One

I love the way you walk and switch your body.
I love the way you talk like a folktale.
I love the way you brush your hair waving
along the waiting shirt on your body.
I love you so much I'm going to love you
until my body gets the chicken pops.
 Don't push don't shove your lover.
I love your bright shining eyes,
they bubble like a rattler.
I love the way you wave your hand
which is saying "Hi Lover."
I love the way you stare at me
like a dog staring at a cat.

 Tony Grant

History

The past
What has happened
before me
before you
before us
The deep knowledge
known to the
nothing
We can only guess
at its knowledge
when there were no cities
no cars
no electricity
Just life
in the age of iron
of medieval soldiers
of time unclassified
or recorded, known
only to stone

Austin Stoker

What does a baby pigeon look like?
Where are all the solid brown cats?
What does a pigeon egg look like?
Where are all the solid gray dogs?
Where is the edge of the ocean?
And is there a gray sky or just gray clouds?
Do you dream in color?
Are memories black and white?
What do you see when you daydream?
What are you looking at?
It's scary when you open your eyes
seeing nothing but darkness.
No matter how you try to see again
it goes black.
That's what it is to be lonely,
to try to hear voices, but hear them
just fade. Something that makes you scared.
You want to come back but don't know how.
And to close your eyes, still see nothing,
open your eyes and see what you once saw again.

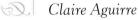

Claire Aguirre

Charm for Money

If you want money go find 2 cacti
1 dead bird
3 fleas
dead man's hair
eye of horse and polluted water.
Put it in a blender and drink it and swim in it
and look into it and say Kum-ba-yah

Money will begin to come to you

A quarter on the street will fly to you
A dollar in a wallet will come to you
Thousands of dollars from a bank vault
will seep out for you through the cracks
You will be the dirtiest crook, the richest crook
and no one can do anything about it
for you will have all power   but don't abuse it
do not take it too far   you will be
      wanted by the ghost
              of
                   money

Gilbert Fernandez

Roller-Skate!

When I roller-skate
    I feel life in a way
    where time is as fast as I am.

When I roller-skate
    I feel power, like being
    superior to the world.

When I turn on my roller skates
    it's like my life changing
    as I grow older.

When I roller-skate
    I feel that loneliness
    cannot catch me.

 Jamshid Afshar, Jr.

Whispers

There is a whisper
of a dog's howl
And the whisper of a night
after a long hard day
And the whisper of a new
fancy office
And the whisper of a day
that surprised everyone
And the whispers that hold
us still while fishing on a
pale lake
And the whisper of a bird
who guards her nest and
flies
  down
    her
      tree
for a worm that looks appealing
And the whisper of an evening
that didn't
t
u r n

out right
And a silence of a whisper during
class
And the whisper of a flag

     W   V   N
       A   I   G

in the wind
And the whisper of a teacher
grading papers

Max H. Wier IV

Ode to Michelangelo's Bones

Many years ago
Michelangelo
Released men
From rocks.

Joe DeLeon

Where does my free time go?
Does it fly off like a shooting star?
Take a trip to the Bahamas?
What if I don't use it?
Does it feel neglected?
Or does it understand?
Is it all-encompassing?
Or know give-and-take?
Does it keep an alarm?
Is it always on time?
Is free time shared by all of us?
I want more.
Hey, free time . . .
You're late.

Karen A. Luk

Finger in a star
    Movie in a star.
    Movie about cowboy
    Cowboy killing Indian.

Finger in a star
    Horse in a star
    Cowboy in the movie
    Indian killing buffalo.

Finger in a star
    Cow in a star
    Cowboy killing sheep killing
    Indian killing buffalo killing
    Cowboy killing Indian killing
    People killing people.

Finger in a star
    Dog killing cat killing rat
    Killing roaches Indian killing
    Cowboy killing buffalo killing
    Sheep killing cowboy killing
    Indian killing people killing
    me.

Gloria Medel

Listen

Listen to the teacher
    when she's not talking.
Listen to the radio
    when it's not on.
Listen to a river
    when it's not flowing.
Listen to yourself
    when you're not listening.

Rene Salazar

Growing is like coming out of the world.
Growing is like kissing the sun.
Growing is like a rose sleeping in a king-size bed.
Growing is like a tree singing to the world.
Growing is like writing better than anyone.
Growing is like to be spotted and not lost.
Growing is like telling the Universe that I am here.

Mary Helen Gonzalez

Where Do They Hide?

My poems hide beneath sands
and under shady trees.
They sit upon river dams
and even laugh at me.
I laugh at them and say,
"You'll never amount to anything."
They say, "Oh, we will someday."

A. R. McMillan

Afterword

Tracking people down to get permission to use their poems is the detective element of every anthology project. This book's search was further complicated by a span of twenty-five years, and the dozens of schools and towns in which I had worked.

Where had all these kids gone? What had happened to them?

A few, thankfully, had stayed known to me—those were easy. Some had unusual names I could trace in the phone directory. A few school districts, teachers, and old friends in various towns offered help. Sometimes I called dozens of phone numbers to locate a single individual. Or not. A "Hays Butler" I located insisted he and his dad were the only two "Hays Butlers" to live in their town during the last four decades, but neither fit the age or school I had, and the one I was talking to swore he had "never been invited to write a poem." "Why not?" he asked petulantly. "Why didn't I get to write a poem?" Some questions I could not answer.

The young poet who had written "Patterns" became a surveyor. The poet who wrote "How to Grow Up" was discovered just as she was lugging boxes from her parents' home to move to a residence of her own in another city. One said, "It's about time! You told me my poem was good enough to get published!" This surprised me. I didn't recall making such reckless promises. I tracked down one startled writer on his cell phone as he stood supervising at a construction site. Another was reading a picture book to his daughter and said, "I read her poems all the time!" Another was out auditioning to be in a play when I phoned long-distance—this made me smile, as I could so clearly remember the charisma he'd had, reading his own poem to the rest of his fourth-grade class.

A few told me they had no memory of their particular poems—a dentist even wrote, "I must tell you I am a very unlikely candidate to be in a poetry anthology." But others said writing and reading poetry had changed their lives irrevocably, that poetry had become their "refuge" after our sessions together, their "private sanctuary" or the place in which they were able to make some sense of the rest of their complicated lives. This made me happy. One invited me to eat at his taco stand. Some signed their permission papers with a flourish, "Long live the muse!"

To all of you, gratitude. To those I didn't find—now it's your turn. Please find me.

Love, Naomi

Acknowledgments

Special thanks to Robert Flynn, who first told me about the writers-in-schools project a quarter century ago; to my old friends at the Texas Commission on the Arts who sponsor so many great programs across the state; to every classroom that encourages creative writing as a crucial, ongoing part of curriculum; to all the teachers and administrators generous enough to share their students with visitors; to Marvin Hoffman, Ron Padgett, Christopher Edgar, and the Teachers and Writers Collaborative for all their heartening, invaluable work with writing and children; to Rosemary Catacalos and Shirley McPhillips, sister-spirits in this long devotion; to Lucy McCormick Calkins and her landmark visionary wisdom with The Teachers College Reading and Writing Project at Columbia University; to Bobby Zamora of the San Antonio Independent School District; Sandee Willis, Betty Law, and Thomas Nye for helping me track down poets; and to artist Ashley Bryan, whose spirit and work I have treasured my whole life. —N. S. N.

Suggestions for Further Reading

The Art of Teaching Writing, by Lucy McCormick Calkins (Portsmouth, N.H.: Heinemann, 1994).

Awakening the Heart: Exploring Poetry in Elementary and Middle School, by Georgia Heard (Portsmouth, N.H.: Heinemann, 1999).

If You Want to Write: A Book About Art, Independence, and Spirit, by Brenda Ueland (Saint Paul, Minn.: Graywolf Press, 1997, first published in 1938).

Learning by Heart: Contemporary American Poetry about School, edited by Maggie Anderson and David Hassler, foreword by Robert Coles (Iowa City, Iowa: University of Iowa Press, 1999).

The Place My Words Are Looking For: What Poets Say About and Through Their Work, selected by Paul B. Janeczko (New York: Atheneum Books for Young Readers, 1990).

Risking Intensity: Reading and Writing Poetry with High School Students, by Judith Rose Michaels (Urbana, Ill.: National Council of Teachers of English, 1999).

Ten-Second Rainshowers: Poems by Young People, compiled by Sandford Lyne (New York: Simon & Schuster Books for Young Readers, 1996).

Today You Are My Favorite Poet: Writing Poems with Teenagers, by Geof Hewitt (Portsmouth, N.H.: Heinemann, 1998).

Writing Across Cultures: A Handbook on Writing Poetry & Lyrical Prose, by Edna Kovacs (Portland, Ore.: Blue Heron Publishing, 1994).

Writing Toward Home: Tales and Lessons to Find Your Way, by Georgia Heard (Portsmouth, N.H.: Heinemann, 1995).

You Must Revise Your Life, by William Stafford (Ann Arbor, Mich.: University of Michigan Press [Poets on Poetry Series], 1986).

In addition to these excellent books, teachers and others interested in creative writing and young people are encouraged to look for the books published by Teachers & Writers Collaborative, 5 Union Square West, New York, NY 10003-3306. *www.twc.org*.

Index to 100 Poems

☙ Waiting for the coffeepot to percolate, one teacher in the lounge speaks to another. "Does poetry have anything to do with math?" Her friend says, "What?" "Well," says the first teacher, "you know how I told you about Benjamin who never does his assignments? So then we started this poetry workshop, he volunteered to read his poems, the other kids cheered him on. Yesterday he brings his math homework in for the first time all year and leaves it on my desk. I don't get it. *What does poetry have to do with math?*"

☙ Caroline lives on a ranch and rides a bus through vast pasturelands to get to her small rural school. Horses bend low in the blowing grasses. Caroline is the first person to get on the bus in the mornings and the last to get off every afternoon, so she writes a lot, in her notebook, in the margins of her homework. She presses her face to the window, stares off across the fields. Today she writes a note to the person who appeared for a few weeks to do creative writing with students at her school. She folds it tightly. *"Thanks for coming to our town. I always knew there must be another poemist out there somewhere."*

The first graders are writing a collaborative poem, fat with dazzling metaphors. Each person adds one line. The visiting poet acts as their scribe, copying what they say in big blue letters on a large white scroll of paper. They will hang it from the ceiling when it's done. Someone has a great idea. "Let's ask Mrs. Nicholas to do the last line!" Mrs. Nicholas has stepped out of the room for a moment. When she returns, her students are bursting with excitement, clapping their hands. "You get to do the last line of the poem!" Her face falls. She shoots the poet an angry look. "No way," she says. "I DON'T WRITE." The silence in the room is sudden and immense.

Salting the Ocean

Index to 100 Young Poets

A fifth-grade boy telephones the poet who visited his class and asks if he could dictate a poem to her. She says, "Umm, why don't you just—write it down yourself and give it to me next week?" He says, "I feel I need to say it into somebody's EAR. Or it won't come out right. There's nobody else at home over here." So she writes down what he says. It's pretty great. She promises to give him a copy next week. Two hours later, her phone rings again. "Do you have another piece of paper?"

≈. An elementary school is having a poetry exhibition, opening after school with a tea party for parents, grandparents, favorite aunts and uncles. Even a few slick brothers and sisters will show up from the high school. There will be music playing in the background, fresh tulips in a big vase on a table. The janitor says he will polish the floor and make it shiny. The cafeteria lady will make sugar cookies to serve. The principal will buy punch. The poets are copying their poems onto large paper. They are illustrating each others' poems. Some want to make mats, so the posters look formal. They plan to dress up and give readings during the opening. The poems will hang in the halls for a whole month. But what will they call their exhibition on the posters and invitations? At least 200 possible titles are nominated. The young poets seem to have an endless appetite for dreaming up titles. The poet visiting their class is listing all the possibilities on the board so they can vote, but the board is full already and her hand is very tired. She says, "Let's turn off the lights and close our eyes and see if the REAL TITLE floats into anybody's head." Lights out. A girl shouts immediately, "QUEEN OF THE RED TOMATOES!" The vote is unanimous.

꩜Brenda erases the last line of her poem about her grandmother many times before turning the poem in. "I think I got it," she says. "And I didn't know what it was—when I started writing. I had to find it."